DISCOVER
The Sound Barrier

by Vickey Herold

Table of Contents

Introduction

People wanted to fly faster. People wanted fast airplanes. People wanted to break the **sound barrier**.

▲ People wanted to fly faster than sound.

Words to Know

dangerous

pilots

rocket engines

sound barrier

speed

supersonic

See the Glossary on page 22.

What Is the Sound Barrier?

The sound barrier is an idea. The sound barrier is an idea about **speed**.

▲ **People do not see the sound barrier.**

The sound barrier is like a wall.

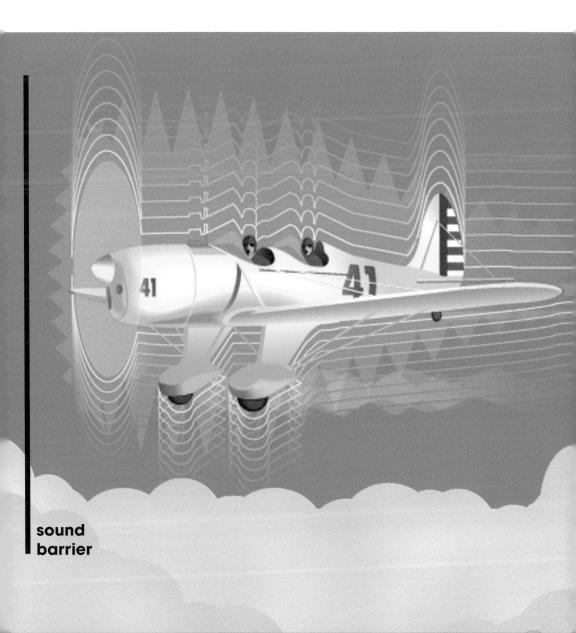

sound
barrier

The sound barrier is 760 miles per hour.

Did You Know?

Many airplanes fly at about 600 miles (966 kilometers) per hour.

▲ Sound travels 760 miles per hour.

The sound barrier is 1,223 kilometers per hour.

▲ **Sound travels 1,223 kilometers per hour.**

What Happened When Airplanes Flew Fast?

Flying fast made airplanes **dangerous**.

▲ Airplanes began to be more dangerous.

Flying fast made airplanes shake.

Flying fast made **pilots** lose control.

▲ Pilots began to lose control.

Flying fast made airplanes crash.

It's a Fact

Airplanes were slow long ago. Airplanes were slower than sound.

▲ Airplanes began to crash.

How Did People Break the Sound Barrier?

People built airplanes that flew faster.

▲ People used faster airplanes.

People built airplanes with **rocket engines**.

▲ **People used rocket engines.**

People built airplanes with a different shape.

▲ People used airplanes with a different shape.

People built airplanes that flew safely.

▲ **People used safer airplanes.**

People built the Bell X-1.

It's a Fact

The Bell X-1 broke the sound barrier. The year was 1947.

▲ People used the Bell X-1.

People built **supersonic** airplanes.

▲ People used supersonic airplanes.

17

Conclusion

People wanted fast airplanes. People wanted airplanes with rocket engines. People wanted to break the sound barrier.

▲ People wanted supersonic airplanes.

Concept Map

The Sound Barrier

What Is the Sound Barrier?

an idea about speed

like a wall

760 miles per hour

1,223 kilometers per hour

What Happened When Airplanes Flew Fast?

made airplanes dangerous

made airplanes shake

made pilots lose control

made airplanes crash

How Did People Break the Sound Barrier?

built faster airplanes

built airplanes with rocket engines

built airplanes with a different shape

built safer airplanes

built the Bell X-1

built supersonic airplanes

Glossary

dangerous not safe

Flying fast made airplanes **dangerous**.

pilots people who fly airplanes

Flying fast made **pilots** *lose control.*

rocket engines rear engines that move objects forward

People built airplanes with **rocket engines**.

sound barrier

sound barrier an air speed of 760 miles per hour (1,223 kilometers per hour)

People wanted to break the **sound barrier**.

speed how fast
something moves

*The sound barrier is an idea
about **speed**.*

supersonic faster than the
speed of sound

*People built **supersonic** airplanes.*

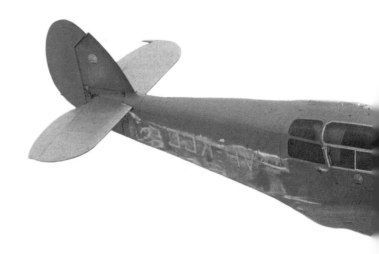

Index